1

Approach to Grief and Grieving

by Jennifer Hancock

The Humanist Approach to Grief and Grieving

by Jennifer Hancock

ISBN-13: 978-1484046579

ISBN-10: 1484046579

The Humanist Approach to Grief and Grieving

by Jennifer Hancock

How to grieve and maintain your sanity

A rational and compassionate approach to bereavement

Other Books by Jennifer Hancock

The Humanist Approach to Happiness: Practical Wisdom

Jen Hancock's Handy Humanism Handbook

The Bully Vaccine

Other Products Available:

The Humanist Approach to Happiness Life Skills Course

The Bully Vaccine Toolkit

Learn more at: www.jen-hancock.com

Acknowledgements

To my daughter Loretta Rose: I still miss you.

To Albert, whose wisdom and willingness to share his own experience with grief was so instrumental in helping my husband and me find the courage to try again.

To everyone who reached out to comfort us in our time of grief and who supported us as we learned to live with our loss. The love you shared provides comfort to me still.

And to everyone who has ever asked me about the Humanist approach to grief, I wrote this book for you.

Table of Contents

Chapter 1: Introduction

Grief is one of the hardest and most profound emotions humans ever experience. At times, it feels like you are losing your mind, and that you will never experience normalcy again. I know. I've been there, having lost a child in the eight month of pregnancy.

While there has been a lot written about grief, not much has been written from an explicitly Humanist perspective. The needs of a Humanist, while grieving, are slightly different from others because Humanists, being rationalists, refuse to allow themselves to be comforted by the false hope of reunion that is a staple of religious belief.

Death is certain. We cannot escape it and as a Humanist, I don't want to. I want to face death and grief with the same courage, compassion and reason that I approach all other aspects of my life.

I decided to write this book to help people who are experiencing grief come to terms with it in a rational and compassionate way. After presiding over my first funeral as a Humanist officiant, I realized that a book on Humanist grief was needed. I felt the pain the bereaved were feeling and I longed to be able to provide them comfort.

I know that Humanism provides an excellent framework for coping with grief, but it is impossible to share all that I know about how Humanists approach grief during a funeral. It also wouldn't do much good even if I could. The bereaved need ongoing support because grief is a process that takes time.

Non-religious individuals who are experiencing grief need a resource that they can turn to as they process their grief. They need a resource that will help them cope, as Humanists, with the emotional trauma that is the grieving process.

This is the book I wish I had been able to give the family that day after I had helped them to bury their father and patriarch. It consists of several essays on grief from a Humanist perspective as well as an excerpt from my book, *The Humanist Approach to Happiness*, from the chapter specifically dealing with grief. Also included are links and information on additional resources you may find handy.

If you are reading this book, there is a good chance you are struggling with grief right now. If that is the case, you have my deepest sympathy. I hope my book helps.

Jen Hancock, Humanist

Chapter 2: A Humanist Prescription for Grief

I am often asked about my personal loss and how the Humanist philosophy helped me through the grieving process. What follows is a simplified version of how I personally approached grief, and what my basic philosophy about the grieving process is.

First – grief isn't something you get over. It is something you learn to live with.

Second - being happy is NOT a betrayal of your grief. If you are grieving, then you, more than anyone else, have earned a little happiness. Don't deny yourself those little moments.

Finally – decide that if you are going to keep on living, you might as well make the best of it. That way – you will allow yourself to be happy when happiness comes.

If you can find a way – once your grief starts to ebb a little – go on outings, take a vacation. It will help remind you what living a happy life is like. The change of scenery should help you recharge your batteries.

Don't feel guilty about choosing life. When you first start grieving, you won't feel up to it. But as time passes, you should experience more and more moments where you are re-engaged with the benefits of living. Don't feel guilty about that. It is what is supposed to happen.

Overcoming Grief

Grief is an incredibly painful emotion. So painful that most of us would rather feel anger or depression than experience it.

The first thing Humanists do after experiencing something traumatic, like the loss of a child, is to make a conscious decision. That decision is to accept our grief in the present with the goal of eventually moving on to live a happy and fulfilling life, despite our loss.

This choice doesn't mean we are planning to avoid our grief or circumvent it. That isn't possible. We simply do not fight it. If we allow ourselves to experience our grief as it comes to us, we know that, over time, we will experience less intense grief and more moments of happiness. And we're OK with that.

What we aren't willing to do is to hold onto our grief indefinitely. We simply experience it and learn to live with it. As rational as this approach seems, I meet people all the time who are working very hard to try and hold on to their grief. I don't see how they do it. Not only is it impossible to feel that intensely all the time, the bigger question is why anyone would want to.

Grief feels horrible. It's not something I would ever choose to experience voluntarily. And yet, some people choose to do just that. And yes, it is a choice. Grief naturally ebbs over time on its own. To maintain high levels of grief, you have to choose to cling to it even as it starts to ebb away. You also have to reject happiness whenever you are fortunate enough to experience it.

After I lost my daughter I decided that since I was going to continue living, I might as well try to be happy - at least part of the time anyway. And no, that's not a betrayal of my grief. The way I looked at it was that if anyone had earned a little happiness, it was me.

I welcomed and celebrated every tiny moment I didn't feel like my world had just ended. I refused to ruin those few seconds of happiness by feeling guilty that I wasn't grieving "acceptably." I knew my grief would return soon enough. It always did. I allowed my grief to ebb and flow. Over time, my grief became less intense and less frequent and my heart had room for joy again - despite my loss.

(Note: The above essay was first published in The Bradenton Herald)

Seeking Help:

Grief is difficult. Everyone grieves differently. The goal of a Humanist is to experience the grief and to eventually find a way back to living life fully. If you find that you are having trouble re-engaging with your life after a year or so, seek out professional help. You will be glad you did.

Chapter 3: Excerpt - The Humanist Approach to Grief

The following chapter is excerpted from my book *The Humanist Approach to Happiness: Practical Wisdom*, and contains the chapter specifically devoted to coping with grief.

Help—I Think I'm Dying!

> *"There were many ways of breaking a heart. Stories were full of hearts broken by love, but what really broke a heart was taking away its dream— whatever that dream might be." - Pearl S Buck*

As with all aspects of life, Humanists approach grief rationally and compassionately. At some point in your life, you will experience grief to a greater or lesser extent. Someone you care about may die, sometimes unexpectedly. You will most likely have your heart broken. Or you may experience some sort of physical trauma. These are all things we know that if we experience them, will cause us to grieve.

There is very little written on the subject of Humanist grief, but what I can tell you is that the Humanist inclination is to approach grief with an eye on the future. Our goal is to survive grief and go on to live a happy and productive life despite our grief. I have spoken to a lot of Humanists on the subject of grief and have been given advice by them to help with my own grieving process, and this really does seem to be the general Humanist approach.

Along these lines, when we Humanists grieve, we try to focus our attention on the fact that our grief is directly related to our happiness. You can see this reflected in Humanist memorial services, where we focus on the life of the deceased and the joy and happiness that individual brought to our lives as a way to deal with our grief.

A basic rule of thumb is that the amount of grief you experience is inversely proportional to the amount of joy what you are grieving gave you. If something gave you a tremendous amount of joy, losing it will cause you a tremendous amount of emotional grief. This is why losing a child is one of the most painful experiences anyone can go through. Painful enough that many marriages don't survive the loss of a child.

Don't Get Me Wrong

> *"The deep pain that is felt at*
> *the death of every friendly soul*
> *arises from the feeling that*
> *there is in every individual*
> *something which is*
> *inexpressible, peculiar to him*
> *alone, and is, therefore,*
> *absolutely and irretrievably*
> *lost." - Arthur Schopenhauer*

Grief is a painful experience, both emotionally and physically, hence the title of this chapter. If you have experienced grief, you will know that you sometimes think you are dying because of it. If the grief is great enough, death might seem like a relief.

Most people might be surprised, though, to realize that grief can also occur for much more benign reasons. The quote at the beginning of this chapter is true. What breaks a heart is taking away its dream. People often grieve changes in lifestyle, even if they wanted to make the change. Changes in jobs, even if good, mean you are leaving a job you might have liked and that all the possibilities of that old job and friendships are now gone. I have grieved to a greater or lesser extent every time I have moved to a new place.

Obviously, when the grief is minimal, it is fairly easy to get through the experience. However, when the grief is great, there are three basic rules to remember to get through the experience without adding additional trauma to an already painful experience: let it flow, let it go, and choose your memories wisely.

Let It Flow

> *"It is some relief to weep; grief is satisfied and carried off by tears. " - Ovid*

The first thing to remember is that grief is an emotion. And, like all emotions, it comes and goes and comes again. Hence, the metaphor, *waves of emotion*. The great thing about emotions, including the painful ones, is that they are temporary. Grief works like any of your other emotions. Once you experience it, your mind will eventually move on to other things and other emotions. So, allow your mind to grieve and let your emotions flow naturally without intellectual interference.

Don't be afraid to experience your emotions. Yes, grief can be incredibly painful. But trying to not experience it won't work. The only thing you will accomplish by trying not to experience the pain of grief is the prolonging of your grief, and why would anyone want to do that? The main problem with trying to avoid grief is that you are always aware of its presence. While you are trying to avoid it you are still experiencing low levels of it. The smarter way to deal with it is to simply experience the waves of grief as they come. I have always found that waves of emotion are actually easier to bear because at least with waves there are breaks from the emotion.

Her Tears Flowed Like Wine

If you need to cry, it is best to let the tears flow. Don't deny yourself this therapeutic urge. If you are grieving something, it is perfectly normal and acceptable to cry. Crying helps purge your body of an overwhelming emotion. You hold tears back at your own risk.

If you need to cry and attempt to stem that tide you will only cause yourself additional grief. Obviously, there are more appropriate times than others to do your crying, but if you feel the need, indulge yourself. You will feel better, even if you are a little embarrassed afterward. Crying will definitely relieve some of your stress.

For major things, such as the death of a child, don't be surprised if you burst out in tears in the supermarket checkout line. You don't have to be strong or hold it in. If anyone has earned the right to cry, it is you.

However, if you are grieving a change in job, you might want to try and schedule your crying time for when you are alone in your own home when no one is watching. Consider it a guilty pleasure.

The important thing to know is that it is physically impossible to cry for very long. Like all emotions, it will come and go. You will eventually stop, even if it is just to fall asleep from exhaustion.

My Advice

Cry if you need to. Don't be embarrassed by it. You have earned the right to cry. But if you are grieving anything less than the death of a loved one, try not to impose your tears on others. In most cases, you should probably try to do your crying in private. The exception is of course when you are offered a shoulder to cry on. Then feel free to go ahead and get your tears and snot on the offered shoulder.

Let It Go

> *"When you are sorrowful look again in your heart, and you shall see that in truth you are weeping for that which has been your delight."* - Kahlil Gibran

If you have experienced something that has caused you to grieve, then you, above all others, have earned a little happiness. Don't deny yourself little rays of happiness in the otherwise turbulent storm of grief.

It is amazing to me how many people hold onto their grief. They don't want to let it flow and let it go for even a few moments. It's as if they think that allowing their emotions to ebb and flow is somehow a betrayal to the depth of feeling they held for what they are grieving. Don't fall into this trap. Grief is an emotion and there is no wrong or right way to experience it. If you smile at a joke or at the sight of a flower, or laugh at how wet your pillow is after a crying jag, it doesn't mean that your emotions weren't real or strong or that you didn't care. It only means that you are allowing your emotions to flow normally without intellectual interference. It means you are an emotionally healthy individual.

Being emotionally healthy, and allowing your emotions to ebb and flow is a good thing. People who practically force their grief onto themselves aren't emotionally healthy. Just as trying to keep grief away doesn't work and is actually counterproductive, trying to keep your grief front and center doesn't work either. Your brain won't let you. If you try, you will end up beating yourself up for failure and that will only make you feel worse, not better. The whole point of grief is to eventually feel better.

Time Heals All Wounds

This normal ebb and flow of grief is why the phrase "time heals all wounds" resonates so well. It isn't that your grief magically disappears at some point in time; it is rather that if you allow your emotions to ebb and flow, eventually you will feel less grief and more happiness. If you try to force your emotions to stay at bay or stay in your face, you are not allowing your natural emotional ebb and flow to occur and aren't, as they say, letting go.

If you are having trouble allowing yourself small moments of happiness then consider this: after all you have been through, haven't you earned a little happiness? Don't deny yourself these small moments of happiness. They are precious and you shouldn't waste them by reprimanding yourself for experiencing them.

My Advice

Emotions are temporary things. They ebb and flow, and it is usually best to allow them to ebb and flow rather than trying to force them into a pattern you think is right. Don't worry about moments of happiness in a sea of grief. If your grief is severe, your grief will return, have no doubt about that. View these small respites as something to be welcomed and eventually you will experience them more frequently and for longer periods of time.

Other Baggage

- *"Anger is never without a reason, but seldom with a good one."*

  - Benjamin Franklin

Grief and sadness aren't the only emotions you will feel during a period of grief. There are a lot of ancillary emotions that come with grief, especially anger and depression. Realize that these are natural emotions to feel and you should allow yourself to experience them. It is important, however, to not get stuck on these emotions. They should ebb and flow as your other emotions do.

The problem is that people often get wrapped up in their grief-related emotions; they attach more importance to them than is normally warranted. When grieving, we all have a tendency to try and make our anger and/or depression the primary emotions we feel. This is understandable because as bad as anger and depression are to experience, they are exponentially less painful than grief. The point you need to remember is to not hold onto your grief-related anger or depression. Let it go and let it flow as you do your other emotions.

Anger

This is especially important with grief-related anger because this sort of anger is often displaced. It is an especially bad idea to actually act on displaced anger. Allow your grief-related anger to ebb and flow and see if it sticks around after the lion's share of the grief has gone away before taking your grief-related anger seriously. The other benefit of allowing your anger to ebb and flow is that once it has ebbed, you will have more perspective on it. Given enough time you may discover that your anger was silly and misplaced.

For Example

When grieving the loss of my daughter, I actually had a lot of anger towards, of all people, a now-famous movie director. It's kind of a long story going back to when I was in high school. The point is he had nothing to do with the death of my daughter. My anger with him was totally misplaced. It was pretty silly really.

A Word About Faith

Faith can be a very contentious thing during periods of grief. I have no doubt that many people find solace in their faith, but for many people faith is a source of anger and conflict during periods of grief.

For those of you, to whom faith is a source of comfort, please be aware that this isn't the case for everyone. Don't assume that what works for you will work for others. And, if you are a person of faith and find yourself becoming angry with God, go back and reread my section about displaced anger.

My Advice

It goes without saying that not acting on grief-related anger is super-doubly important if you are grieving a broken heart. Don't act on your anger until you are over your grief. Just don't. Let it go and congratulate yourself on how mature you are being despite your overwhelming urges to seek revenge. Keep reminding yourself that you are an ethical, compassionate, and responsible person and that you aren't the sort to do something irrational or stupid.

Memories

> *"That which is dreamed can
> never be lost, can never be
> undreamed." - Master Li (in
> Neil Gaiman's Sandman comic)*

It is wrong to think that you will or should get over your grief. It is more accurate to say that you will eventually learn to live with the loss. If you allow yourself to grieve and allow your emotions to ebb and flow, you will eventually integrate that loss into your life and while it may still be sad, it won't be quite as painful. Eventually you will be able to get on with your life and be able to do everyday things such as shopping without bursting out crying at the sappy song playing on the radio.

The best way to integrate a loss into your life is to seek out happy memories. Your memories of whatever it is you lost will be what remain, and you need to find a place for them. Try to make the memories you focus on happy ones. That way, when you do find yourself reminiscing, it will bring you a melancholy joy and not as much pain and sadness.

While this last bit of advice is good, it is only partially applicable to the grief of a broken heart. Too many happy thoughts about a relationship that ended might encourage you to seek your ex out, and that is a bad idea. You are no longer together for a reason. What is broken up should stay broken up. On the other hand, if several years after you had your heart broken, you are still getting angry and sad and upset when you think of your ex, you need to try something else, and I would suggest that something else should be professional counseling.

The Humanist Approach to Grief

> *"If you're going through hell, keep going." - Winston Churchill*

While grief is indeed painful, Humanists view it as a normal part of life. It is not something you should run from, but neither should you suffer from it unnecessarily. The goal of the Humanist is to be happy and so we approach our grief rationally and compassionately. We allow ourselves to grieve and to find happiness in our grief and eventually let go of the grief so that we can live fully in our futures.

Grief is painful, but it is an emotion and emotions ebb and flow. Allow yourself to grieve, but don't hold onto your grief either. Allow yourself to find moments of happiness and eventually you will feel less pain and more happiness.

After the death of my daughter, I joined a few grief support groups specifically for people who had lost children. I wasn't too surprised to find that most people put too much pressure on themselves during times of grief. Most were concerned about their level of grief. Were they grieving too much? Not enough? Don't worry about those things. Everyone grieves differently. How you grieve is right for you. Do some research and learn what the experts on grief have to say. Most of all, be prepared for your emotions to be all over the place and be compassionate with yourself.

The thing that really amazed me, as I participated in these grieving groups, was how many people refused to be happy or to seek happiness after the loss of a loved one. It was like they felt that being happy was somehow a betrayal of the person they had lost. That concept is really lost on a Humanist. Perhaps it is our rationality that helps us through. But as far as I am concerned, if there is such a thing as sin, suffering must be a sin. Sometimes you can't avoid suffering. But it seems to me it would be better to be happy. If you are planning to continue living despite your loss, it would probably be a good idea to at least try to get on with being happy.

When it comes to grief; this simple inescapable truth is what motivates a Humanist in our times of grief: since we plan to go on living because we like being alive, we might as well be happy. We have nothing to be ashamed of in taking this approach. It is rational, compassionate, and responsible. We don't hide from the pain of grief. Instead we choose to view it as a reflection of the joy and love we feel from what we lost.

Chapter 4: Meditations

This chapter includes three short meditations on different aspects of coping with grief and the stress that comes with it.

How Humanists Cope with stress – why not me?

We all know bad things happen to even the nicest of people. But how exactly do Humanists cope with stressful situations, especially since we do not rely on supernatural assistance to help us handle life's difficulties?

I know a thing or two about struggling with tragedy. Over the years I have had to deal with a stalking and with the loss of a child. My Humanism helped me cope successfully with both situations.

When faced with a stressful or upsetting situation, the first thing most people ask is "why me?" Our answer to this question is "why not me?" People were stunned when Christopher Hitchens said exactly this in an interview when he was first diagnosed with cancer. But that is honestly how we

Humanists answer this question. As one of my friends noted, we find comfort in our insignificance. We know there is nothing special about us that will immunize us from tragedy.

As horrid as this may seem, we Humanists feel it is far better to accept reality then to delude ourselves into thinking we were special and should have been spared. From a Humanist perspective, all believing you are special does is add unnecessary baggage to an already painful situation. We really don't understand why anyone would do that to themselves.

The second thing people do when coping with stress is to try to escape from what is happening. This can be a mental escape or a physical escape, but we humans seem to prefer magical escapes. Humanists are not immune to these urges. After all, the idea that we could magically be delivered from our trauma is extremely attractive. Unfortunately, the world doesn't work that way.

Humanists accept that there is only one way through what we are going through, and that is to get through it. This approach does require you to be rational at a time when your emotions are screaming for relief. It also requires you to accept that it is your responsibility to cope. No one else can do that for you.

We understand why people take comfort in faith in difficult times. We just think that ultimately, it is our responsibility to do the heavy emotional lifting ourselves. Attempting to take shortcuts through this process will only prolong our pain. That is not something we would rationally choose to do.

Humanists discipline themselves to confront these sorts of challenges by deciding first and foremost that we will get through it. After all, if we are going to keep on living, we don't really have a choice. Supernaturalism is unnecessary. Our desire is to not only live, but to be happy. This gives us all the courage we need to confront our problems head on.

(Note: The above essay first appeared in The Bradenton Herald)

Death isn't depressing

Well, ok, yes it is, but only when it happens to others. When someone we love and care about dies, it saddens us. We will no longer be able to spend time with or talk to our friend. We experience that loss as grief. However, when we think about our own death, it doesn't necessarily have to depress us. It all depends on how you approach it.

At some point, all of us will die, unless we experience a singularity that allows us to live forever. I'm not holding my breath on that. I'd like to live for a few hundred years, but that isn't realistic at this time.

I accept that at some point I will die and miss out on everything that will occur after my death. And yeah, that is a little depressing. But here is how the average Humanist turns that around.

Knowing that we are eventually going to die makes life precious to us. We have a finite amount of time to live. It would be a shame to waste it. This is why a huge part of what it means to be a Humanist is to live life to the fullest. This is a choice we make and yes, it means we are living life intentionally too. You can't live life fully unless you live it intentionally.

Don't think about death as a depressing thing. Instead, use the knowledge of death to spur you to embrace life fully in the here and now.

Grief Returns

If you have lost a loved one, you know certain times of the year can be very hard: like anniversaries, birthdays, and holidays. Years afterward when you rarely think of it anymore, there it comes, out of the blue, renewed grief.

It happened to me one day while I was driving my son to daycare. As I was thinking about the color of my son's eyes I realized that I didn't know what color my daughter's eyes were. My emotions overwhelmed me and I suddenly felt as horrible as I had at her funeral. I cried right then and there.

Because I know that it is perfectly normal for this sort of thing to happen. I allowed myself my tears and laughed at the displaced anger that was cropping up.

Don't be afraid of your grief. Experiencing it means you are normal and alive. And believe it or not, that is something to celebrate.

Chapter 5: Children and Grief

Children and grief

As a Humanist parent I am often asked about how to talk to a child about death without a) making a huge deal out of it

b) how to keep it in a natural as opposed to supernatural context, and

c) how to help a child cope with grief in the absence of supernatural comforting.

My son lost one of his grandfathers when he was 3 years old, so I had to deal with this way earlier than I was prepared for. I have to admit, I choked for a few days and hesitated telling him. I knew I needed to but my husband had flown to Tennessee to be with his mom and to help her with the funeral. I didn't want to be alone with an inconsolable child. I was afraid. It turns out I needn't have been.

When I finally mustered up the courage, I did what came naturally: I was honest with him. I didn't use any metaphors; I just told him what had happened and that he wouldn't be seeing his grandfather anymore. It turns out this is considered a best practice for talking to kids about death. It is important you use the word death and don't substitute a metaphor as that can confuse a young child. Their grandparent went away? Where? Will they see them again? Why not? Death is death. It is easier for the child if we don't hide it from them.

My son took the news quite well. However, he had a lot of questions about it and by a lot I mean, he was asking questions about death for about two years off and on. At first it worried me that my son had become death obsessed, but that is not what was going on. It turns out that truly understanding death isn't all that easy. We adults have problems coming to terms with death. It isn't any easier for a child. In fact, coming to terms with death really is a lifelong process. Death isn't something you can explain or grasp in a single conversation. Kids require several small conversations over a period of years to help them figure it out.

My son cried quite a bit and still does whenever he thinks of his grandfather. However, we had a big breakthrough when he was 5, when one of our cats died. This time he grieved properly. He went through all the stages of grief from denial to bargaining. It was hard to watch him experience grief, but we knew that if we tried to ease his pain, we would be denying him an important opportunity to experience one of the most painful and yet most profound emotional experiences we humans can have.

The quickest way through grief is to just experience it. We did not allow him to take detours with false hopes that the dead cat would resurrect, be replaced or be seen again in an afterlife. Having gone through this experience, he has a much better understanding of death, but more importantly, he isn't afraid of it either. People and animals he has loved have died, and life goes on. Yes, it is sad and we will always miss them, but at least we got to know and love them when they were alive.

Humanistic parenting is respectful, honest, and compassionate. Our goal is to prepare our children for life, the good and the bad. We know if we shield them from the unpleasantness of life, they will not be prepared to cope emotionally. Our job as parents is to help our child practice and learn adaptive coping skills in a compassionate and respectful way. Learning to cope with death, as unpleasant as it is, is something our kids need to learn. When the inevitable happens, help your children through their grief, don't shield them from it.

The Death of a cat

The death of a pet is an excellent opportunity to help your child learn about death and learn positive coping skills. When one of our cats died, it turned out to be a very good experience for my son even though it was quite sad.

Sally was a very beautiful cat. She looked like a Russian Blue/Dilute Torti mix. She was seriously a beautiful cat. Too bad she rarely let anyone pet her. That is, up until the end. As she neared the end of her life, she started to come out more and she even allowed my son to pet her and give her love. He was thrilled!!!

Then she died. And he cried. Grief follows very similar processes regardless of who died. We feel the same grief over the death of a cat as we do for a human. The only difference is varying intensity.

To help our son, we obviously did not tell him he is going to see Sally again. The urge to ease his pain was strong, but we resisted as we felt that would do more harm than good. We also refused to replace her with another pet as that would only divert his grief. She couldn't be replaced and forcing him to face the reality of her death, as cruel as that might seem, is what allowed him to experience his grief and eventually come to terms with it.

Like nearly everyone who has lost a loved one, he at first tried to deny our cat's death by hoping she would resurrect and then when that wasn't an option, he hoped she could re-incarnate. He cried a lot and was sad. We told him he would never forget her and that it was ok to be sad and to cry. Three days later he was done crying. He would mention that he missed her in passing but he had basically gotten on with the business of living his life. He didn't even cry himself to sleep that night as he preferred to discuss our plans for the weekend.

Grief in a nutshell.

Deny it, come to terms with it, feel bad about it and then get on with your life never forgetting the one you loved and lost.

Chapter 6: Getting Help

In this chapter, you will find several essays that address different ways to find help with your grief. The needs of Humanists and other non-religious individuals is different from that of people of faith. What comforts a person of faith will often be quite hurtful to a non-religious individual.

This chapter includes information on how to comfort the non-religious, secular funerals, why the god concept is so problematic for Humanists who are grieving, and how and why Humanist celebrants provide non-religious funeral services.

Comforting the non-religious

A while back my local paper ran a column where a reporter asked two different faith leaders questions about various religious issues. One question was about how to comfort a grieving person who lacks faith. The answers came from pastors of a Catholic Church and a Unity Church. They should have asked a Humanist Celebrant what we who lack faith need while grieving. Certainly, someone who lacks faith is more knowledgeable about this subject than someone who believes.

While the Catholic response was quite nice and compassionate, the Unity pastor was so off base it actually brought up painful memories of the offensive things I was told by well-meaning people of faith after I lost my daughter. I understand that these people were trying to provide comfort, but the things that comfort a religious person often just annoy a non-religious person and sometimes can be quite offensive.

For the record, we who lack faith aren't at all worried about the fate of the dead. They are dead. They no longer have a fate to be concerned about. We aren't worried about whether they are in heaven or hell or whether they turned into a ghost or not. These are religious and supernatural concepts and we aren't religious and we reject supernaturalism. Instead, we focus on how we as survivors are going to cope with our loss and continue on without our loved ones in our lives. Humanist memorial ceremonies, as a result, serve to help us remember or memorialize the deceased as we celebrate their life. But just as important is that Humanist memorials focus on the needs of the survivors as they start their grief journey.

After a loss, what we need is for people to acknowledge our grief and let us know they care and that we will be supported as we learn to live with our loss.

Secular Funerals

If you are not already familiar with a Humanist funeral, here is some information about Humanist memorial services.

Having participated in both religious and non-religious memorials, I like the Humanist memorials much better. The religious elements of traditional memorials are very distracting, unnecessary and confusing to me. I would rather focus on my grief and sorrow and remember the dead than try to sort out a particular cleric's beliefs about the afterlife.

Humanist memorials are quite moving, specifically because they are designed for the living. A Humanist memorial service helps the survivors come to terms with the death of their friend and/or loved one. By remembering their life you celebrate the impact they had on yours. You have an opportunity to say goodbye (an opportunity you may not have had otherwise.) In short, they help the living come to terms with their loss.

Because most Humanists are non-religious, and therefore don't believe in an afterlife, there is no need to help the deceased navigate their way to heaven or hell or wherever people might go to when they die. Even if there is a heaven or hell, it is highly unlikely that a memorial service will have an impact on the routing of the deceased anyway, so the focus is on helping the living. Further, if the deceased wasn't a religious person, then to give them a religious memorial simply because some of the surviving family members might want it would be like insulting the very individual you are supposed to be memorializing. Why not respect them and remember them for who they were and not who you wanted them to be.

It is very selfish of someone to dictate his or her religious needs on others. You might want a religious ceremony for yourself, but if others don't want or need that, then you should respect that. If you are truly going to honor and respect the dead, then don't have a religious memorial service for a non-religious individual.

Grief and God

There is a very common assumption that belief in god(s) and/or an afterlife makes grieving easier. After all, without belief in an afterlife, there can be no hope that you will ever see your loved one again. Having lost a child myself, I sympathize with the desire for death to not be real or final. However, wanting my child to still be alive and hoping that I might actually get to see her again is a fantasy. It is a fantasy that, most Humanists feel, is harmful to the grieving process.

I don't believe that it is important for people to turn to God during times of crisis. I realize I am coming to this as a religious outsider and there are plenty of good clergy who chose a life of ministry because they really do care, but ... there is a reason why I think religious belief does more harm than good during times of grief. All religion seems to offer people who are grieving is a story that assures the listener that death isn't real and that the person, who died, didn't really die. Humanists don't view these sorts of "afterlife" stories as comforting. We view them as harmful. Here is why.

As comforting as it might be to believe that you will see a loved on again. All a belief in an afterlife does is offer the grieving a convenient way to defer or avoid grief. It doesn't help anyone come to terms with it. In order to come to terms with grief, you have to experience it and that means you have to accept the reality of death, not avoid it or pretend it isn't real.

No one can help you overcome your grief. It is something you have no choice but to experience. Yes, there are people who can help you learn how to process your emotions more effectively, but you are actually better off seeking a professional grief counselor than going to someone who offers you magical solutions to your grief problem.

Here is another reason why religious belief makes grieving harder, not easier. Religious belief causes extra stress and heartache to the bereaved.

When I lost my daughter, I was heartbroken. My husband and I grieved and still do. However, as we processed our grief and joined support groups, we noticed that we seemed to be the only ones who were just experiencing grief. We didn't have any baggage on top of our grief to deal with. At no point did we ask "why us?" We did not have to wrestle with our beliefs or question the very nature of "god." We just grieved, and knew from experience and from our readings on the subject that our pain would ease over time, which it did.

I really think that not having to wrestle with the question of "why us" during our grief was a great relief. There are many people, however, who do wrestle with these questions and they overwhelmingly are people that believe they have a personal relationship with their god. If you have come to believe that out of the entire 7 billion plus humans on the planet you are special and will be spared the pain of grief then when, not if, you experience a loss, you won't just experience the pain of grief. You will also experience the disorientation of having your world turned upside down. And from what I gather, that isn't pleasant. It is a heavy load that is added to an already overburdened mind.

For my husband and me, knowing that there wasn't anything special about us was actually comforting. Our acceptance of science told us that there was a chance of losing our child despite all the advancement of medicine. And while it is horrid to be a statistic, we know that there is nothing about us that would have spared us from this experience. That is just the luck of the draw. Sometimes things just happen. We just happened to lose our daughter, as many others have before us.

I am now firmly convinced that our non-belief made our grief easier to handle. We saw what people of faith were going through and it seemed to be unnecessarily more painful than it needed to be simply because they weren't just grieving the loss of their child. They were also wrestling with personal demons arising from their presumed relationship with "god." Grief is hard enough. Adding unnecessary baggage makes grief harder, not easier, to deal with.

The role of celebrants in helping people during times of grief

I am not trained nor certified as a celebrant, though I probably should be. I'm great at public speaking. I love to talk about Humanism. I volunteer for all sorts of activities in an effort to make the world a better place. But being a celebrant requires you to be intimate during the most significant events of a stranger's life. From the birth of a baby to a wedding or a funeral, it is during the most emotional moments of joy and grief that Humanist celebrants are needed. The reason I haven't become a celebrant, to be perfectly honest, is because I'm scared.

Even though I am a public speaker, some situations make me nervous. To be a central figure in the emotional events of the lives of complete strangers seemed too much for me. I wasn't sure if I could handle it or if I even wanted to handle it.

One evening I received a call to help with the funeral of a stranger. Their father had died and they hadn't been able to find a celebrant to help them, and by the way, the funeral was the very next day. I had to make a decision. Is my personal insecurity and fear more important than assisting with the grief of a stranger? Was I willing to give up a relaxing weekend with my family to spend the day with people who had just lost their father?

Funerals aren't planned the way weddings are. They come suddenly, and the family has less than a week to find someone to deliver a service that will both comfort them and provide a worthy tribute to the person they lost.

I agreed to help. Not because I knew what I was doing, but because no one should have to go through what they went through. In addition to their grief, they had the added burden of finding someone secular to deliver the service. All the local celebrants were out of town, and they were desperate to avoid hiring a religious individual because they did not want their father to have a religious service because they did not want to hear that they would see him again because they knew they wouldn't. This was not a religious family and the father they had lost was not a religious man. He was a Humanist, a scientist, and a world traveler. He was the sort of man I would have loved to have known. A man who had a small scale replica of the Rosetta Stone on his desk.

I learned a lot by putting aside my fears to help someone in need that day. I learned I can handle it. Yes, my voice was shaking as I started my service. But I also felt good. Helping people, real people, who truly need my support, is one of the most important things I can do. It is when we are helping others that we feel like we are living our lives as we should. This is the goal of every Humanist: to live life fully and intentionally, helping to make life easier for not just ourselves, but for others as well.

What better way to do that than to minister to those who need comfort in their time of grief. And yes, I did just say minister, because that is what I did that day. I administered aid and comfort. Having done this, I now realize just how important it is to be a celebrant. It is probably one of the noblest expressions of our philosophy: to rise to the challenge and not just talk about helping real people, but to actually help.

The number of people who are secular in this country is growing. Most are not involved with organized Humanist groups. They are busy going about their lives. But when they have a child, or a wedding, or a funeral, they need someone who can help them celebrate and/or grieve in a way that is consistent with their beliefs and values.

I never realized exactly how important celebrants are. That's because I never provided celebrant services myself. What this family went through isn't uncommon. The funeral director said he gets requests for secular funerals all the time but that he doesn't have anyone he can refer people to. I'm still very emotional about this because panicking about whether or not a funeral service will be consistent with your values is not something anyone should have to deal with when they are grieving.

We who are active in the Humanist movement, need to step up and be there for these people. We need to overcome our fears and offer ourselves in service to complete strangers, even when it is inconvenient as most funerals are.

I have had no training as a celebrant. All I had was a book, *Funerals without God*, which is little more than a pamphlet. Using that as my guide, I was able to create a memorial service that honored the life of a man I wish I had been given the opportunity to know. My delivery wasn't very good because I was so emotional while I was delivering it. It turned out that more important than my skill, was the fact that I was there at all.

Humanist funerals are unique. Our approach is to celebrate the life of the deceased and to focus on helping the survivors come to terms with death. Because our approach is both compassionate and personalized, it works. You don't have to be perfect; you just have to be willing to be human. If you have ever thought of becoming a celebrant, now is the time. Don't wait, the need is too great. You can learn how to do this by reading books and by talking to other celebrants. Just make sure your local funeral parlors know you are available.

Suicide

One of the big topics relating to grief is the issue of suicide. The average Humanist's response to suicide is:

Don't commit suicide!

Life is amazing. And yes, it is hard at times, and painful, and sad at times. And believe me, I know. I have lost a child and been the victim of a stalking. I have known sadness and pain so powerful that it is incapacitating. I have known fear so intense it is immobilizing. But those are just emotions. Regardless of how intense they are, they are temporary and can be overcome. I am living proof that it is possible to not just overcome them but to thrive. It's hard, but it can be done.

The question people considering suicide often ask is, "why not just kill myself and get it over with?" Humanists find this question to be a very unsatisfying and depressing question to ask. It has no good answer. If you find yourself asking that question, stop.

The better question to ask yourself is this. "Despite it all, why not live?" Go on. Ask yourself this question and see how you feel afterwards, I'll wait. …. To even ask that question is in some ways an act of defiance. It feels good. More importantly, even a halfhearted response to "why not live" opens up a new world of possibilities.

The Humanist approach is to live despite it all. And not only to live but to embrace life whole-heartedly: the good and the bad, and to ultimately be happy. Life is amazing and hard, but it is life and life is to be lived. And if you die, you will miss it all, and that would be a shame.

If you are suffering from depression and are thinking of killing yourself, don't. Go to your doctor and tell them you are depressed and be honest with them about exactly how depressed you really are. They really can help you and you will feel much better once you are honest with someone else about how badly you have been feeling. If you can't afford a doctor or don't have one, go to your county health clinic and tell someone there about how you feel. Help is available, go and get it.

Suicide is often an impulsive decision. Don't be impulsive about the most important decision of your life. Seek professional help instead.

Check out – http://www.suicidepreventionlifeline.org *for more information*

Chapter 7: Resources

Grief is a process that takes time, and you will need help as you process your emotions. Here is a list of resources that may come in handy.

Secular Celebrants

The first area people need help in is finding a celebrant to provide a non-religious funeral for the deceased.

If you are in the USA, there are two groups that certify celebrants.

The American Humanist Association's Humanist Society at http://humanist-society.org/celebrants/ which has a list of celebrants around the country and

The Council for Secular Humanism which has their list of celebrants at:

http://www.secularhumanism.org/index.php?section=library&page=celebrants_14_1

The congregation of Humanistic Judaism has trained Humanist rabbi's who can perform Humanist or secular funerals for you as well.
http://www.humanisticrabbis.org/rabbis-in-north-america/

You may also find ministers at a Unitarian Universalist congregation who are willing and able to provide a secular funeral. If you are lucky enough to live near an Ethical Culture Society, they can also provide secular funerals.

If you are in the UK, the British Humanist Association maintains a list of celebrants at:
http://humanism.org.uk/ceremonies/find-a-celebrant/

And the Humanist Society of Scotland has their list at: http://www.humanism-scotland.org.uk/content/celebrants/

Australia's Humanist Celebrant Network is at:
http://www.humanistcelebrantnetwork.org/

Finally, if you are in another country, find your country's Humanist association. They should have a list of celebrants local to you.
http://iheu.org/geography

Grief Support Groups and professional counseling

Once the rush of the funeral is over, you will find that you will now have no distractions from your grief. It is at this point that you will benefit from finding a grief support group or the assistance of a professional grief counselor. Here are some non-religious options for you to consider:

If you are looking for a grief support group, but don't know where to turn, I suggest you join Grief Beyond Belief on Facebook.
http://www.facebook.com/faithfreegriefsupport

The Association for Humanistic Psychology has a list of Humanistic Psychologists who should be able to help you with your grief if you find you are stuck or having problems: http://www.ahpweb.org/

Also be sure to check with your local Humanist group to see if it offers any grief support. Most don't, but some do, so you may get lucky. If you have no grief support group, consider starting one of your own.

Books

There are only a couple of books which specifically deal with the topic of grief from a Humanist or non-religious perspective:

Raising Freethinkers by Dale McGowan has excellent information – especially if you are helping a child cope with grief. There are other topics covered in this book as well, but the section of grief is outstanding.

Funerals Without God by Jane Wynne Wilson is a practical guide to non-religious funerals. It is what I used to put together my first funeral service.

There are several excellent books written by Humanistic Psychologists or people trained in the cognitive behavioral model which is a form of Humanistic Psychology. One of the top recommended books is: *The Grief Recovery Handbook* by John James and Russell Friedman.

Other online grief support material you may find useful

Top 10 humanist grief songs:
http://www.youtube.com/watch?v=u2RygYa571l

Officiating Grief:
http://harvardhumanist.org/2012/01/24/officiating-grief/

Grief Beyond Belief:
http://www.secularhumanism.org/index.php?section=fi&page=hensler_32_5

Death and Grief from Humanist Resources:
http://www.humanistresources.org/topics/death-grief

Grief and Loss worksheets and other tools
http://www.psychologytools.org/grief.html

Am I grieving Right?
http://societyforhumanisticpsychology.blogspot.com/2012/01/am-i-grieving-right-we-pay-price-when.html

The Good Grief Project at Boston Medical Center:
http://bmc.org/pediatrics-goodgrief.htm

The Grief Recovery Blog:
http://www.griefrecoverymethod.com/blog/#

Grief Loss and Bereavement:
http://www.goodtherapy.org/therapy-for-grief.html

Children and Grief:
http://www.childgrief.org/childrenandgrief.htm

Dealing with death in a secular family:
http://www.the-brights.net/action/activities/organized/arenas/2/parenting/DealingWithDeath.pdf

Chapter 8: About the Author

 Jennifer Hancock is a Humanist Life Skills educator. She helps transform people's lives by teaching people how Humanism can help them in all aspects of their life, and how it can help them to be the best most ethical person they can be.

Her work focuses on three key areas:

- How to make better decisions through critical thinking.

- How to improve your relationships through compassion.

- How to infuse your life with meaning and purpose by prioritizing your ethics.

By sharing her pragmatic Humanist approach to living life fully and intentionally, Jennifer has transformed the lives of those who have been touched by her work. By encouraging people to be the best, most ethical humans they can be, she consistently challenges people to think about and question who they are, what they are and more importantly, how they want to be. Her work encourages people to rise to the challenge of living fully: embracing both the good and the bad as part of what it means to be alive.

What is Humanism?

Humanism is a highly effective approach to human development. It is as concerned with personal development as it is with social responsibility. It is probably the most humane and holistic approach to ethical philosophy humanity has ever devised.

Other books and programs by Jennifer Hancock

Living Made Simpler: A Humanist Life Skills Course

This six-week course is designed to teach you the basic life skills Humanists use to lead happy, fulfilling, and productive lives and how best to cope with stress and other challenges. What this course will do is provide you with the skills to better implement and live by the values you already hold, empower you to be a better person, and provide you with hints and tips on how to overcome the obstacles we all have to deal with throughout our lives that make it hard to be the best, most ethical person you can be. Learn more at http://humanisthappiness.com

The Humanist Approach to Happiness: Practical Wisdom

This is a book that basically says: Here are personal ethics, here is why they are important, and here is how you can apply them to your daily life and why doing so will help you live a happier more productive life. Life isn't easy. It is filled with challenges. How we navigate those challenges determines our success in life. If you want to learn more about how to think more effectively about the choices you make, this book will help. Learn more at: http://happiness.jen-hancock.com/

Jen Hancock's Handy Humanism Handbook

This book is written to provide a quick overview of the philosophy of Humanism for the average human who wants to learn more about Humanism. Humanism is one of the most influential and yet most maligned philosophies of all time. Unfortunately, most people don't know anything about it. To make matters worse, there are a lot of people who are already Humanists and just don't know it yet because no one has ever taken the time to properly introduce them to the philosophy. Consider yourself introduced. Learn more at: http://www.jen-hancock.com/handyhumanism/

The Bully Vaccine

This book is designed to help parents vaccinate their kids against bullies and other obnoxious petty people. By preparing for them in advance you can effectively inoculate yourself against the worst of their behavior. The technique and tools taught in the book are based on operant conditioning. In other words, I will teach you how to train your bully to leave you alone. And yes, it really does work. Learn more at: http://thebullyvaccine.com

Where to find Jen online:

Twitter: https://twitter.com/#!/JentheHumanist

Facebook:
http://www.facebook.com/JentheHumanist

Youtube: http://www.youtube.com/user/Sumogirl1

Google+:
https://plus.google.com/105203791195680352003/posts

Join my mailing list: http://eepurl.com/c3LuI

Made in the USA
Middletown, DE
07 March 2015